The Oxford Piano Method

P·I·A·N·O T·I·

T0087066

GOING PLACES

Pauline Hall and Korky Paul

MUSIC DEPARTMENT

OXFORD
UNIVERSITY PRESS

OXFORD
UNIVERSITY PRESS

Great Clarendon Street, Oxford OX2 6DP, England
198 Madison Avenue, New York, NY10016, USA

Oxford University Press is a department of the University of Oxford.
It furthers the University's aim of excellence in research, scholarship,
and education by publishing worldwide

Oxford is a registered trade mark of Oxford University Press
in the UK and in certain other countries

Illustrations © Korky Paul 2003

© Oxford University Press 2003

The moral rights of the authors and illustrator have been asserted
Database right Oxford University Press (maker)

First published 2003

All rights reserved. No part of this publication may be reproduced,
stored in a retrieval system, or transmitted, in any form or by any means,
without the prior permission in writing of Oxford University Press,
or as expressly permitted by law. Enquiries concerning reproduction
outside the scope of the above should be sent to the Music Copyright
Department, Oxford University Press, at the address above

Permission to perform the works in this anthology in public
(except in the course of divine worship) should normally be obtained
from the Performing Right Society Ltd. (PRS), 29/33 Berners Street,
London W1T 3AB, or its affiliated Societies in each country throughout
the world, unless the owner or the occupier of the premises
being used holds a licence from the Society

Permission to make a recording must be obtained in advance
from the Mechanical Copyright Protection Society Ltd. (MCPS),
Elgar House, 41 Streatham High Road, London SW16 1ER,
or its affiliated Societies in each country throughout the world

22

ISBN 978-0-19-372730-4

Music and text origination by
Barnes Music Engraving Ltd., East Sussex
Printed in Great Britain on acid-free paper by
Halstan & Co. Ltd., Amersham, Bucks.

Contents

Beep! beep!	4
Treading carefully	5
Balloon ride	6
Michael, row the boat ashore	7
Cossack dance	8
Hong Kong ferry	9
Take a walk	10
Hop it!	11
Flannagan's jig	12
Bluemerang	13
Mission in space	14
Contrary motion in space and time!	15
Flying above the clouds	16
Let sleeping sharks lie	17
Cycle ride	18
Rollerblade rag	19
Chopsticks with a twist	20
Honk! honk!	21
Penny-farthing	22
A swim in crocodile river	23
Mexican march	24
Paris promenade	25
The train	26
Santa Lucia	27
New Orleans	28
The bluebottle's last journey	29
Two in tandem	30

Beep! beep!

Imagine you are beeping your horn at someone and are getting quite angry. Really jab at those left hand cross-over notes!

Fiona Macardle

As fast as you can

ff

LH

LH

LH

RH

LH

LH

LH

RH

Treading carefully

Alan Haughton

Cautiously

p

mp

mf

8va

f

mf

rit.

loco

mp

p

Balloon ride

Michael, row the boat ashore

American folk tune

On the move

Mich - ael, row the boat a - shore, Hal - le - lu -

mf

-jah, Mich-ael, row the boat a - shore, Hal - le - lu - jah. Sis - ter,

f

help to trim the sail, Hal - le - lu - jah, sis - ter, help to trim the

Slower

sail, Hal - le - lu - jah.

mp

p

Cossack dance

Denis McCaldin

With great energy

𝄋 (last time: faster)

f

(*f*)

simile

1.

2.

Fine

p

1.

2.

D.S. al Fine

Hong Kong ferry

There are no white keys in this piece,
so keep your hands well up over the black keys.

Pauline Hall

Take a walk

Alan Haughton

Hop it!

Not too fast

Alan Haughton

mf

p

mf

p

f

p

sfz

Flannagan's jig

Alan Haughton

Lively

f

mp

cresc.

f

cresc.

ff

Bluemerang

To Australia and back

Alan Haughton

Boogie

mf

mp

f

8va

mp

mf

p

Mission in space

Alan Haughton

Fast

f

2nd time **to Coda** ⊕

p

cresc.

f

D.C. al Coda

⊕ **CODA**

Contrary motion in space and time!

There are only black keys here, so keep your fingers ready to play them!

Slow and steady

Roderick Skeaping

f

Five! Four! Three! Two! One!

Ze - ro! and Blast Off!

Go - ing on a year - long trip to dis - tant stars at speed of light,

If we don't get lost in space-time see you next last Thurs-day night!

Flying above the clouds

Alan Bullard

Let sleeping sharks lie

David Cullen

Slow swing (♩ = 86)

pp *p* *mf*

pp *p*

mf *ff*

Cycle ride

Mark Andrews

Cheerful (♩ = 144, or more!)

mf

mp

f

(*sempre f*)

mf

f

Rollerblade rag

Alan Haughton

Steadily

mf

mp

mf

cresc.

f

Chopsticks with a twist

Fiona Macardle

As fast as possible, with heavy accents where marked

Fine

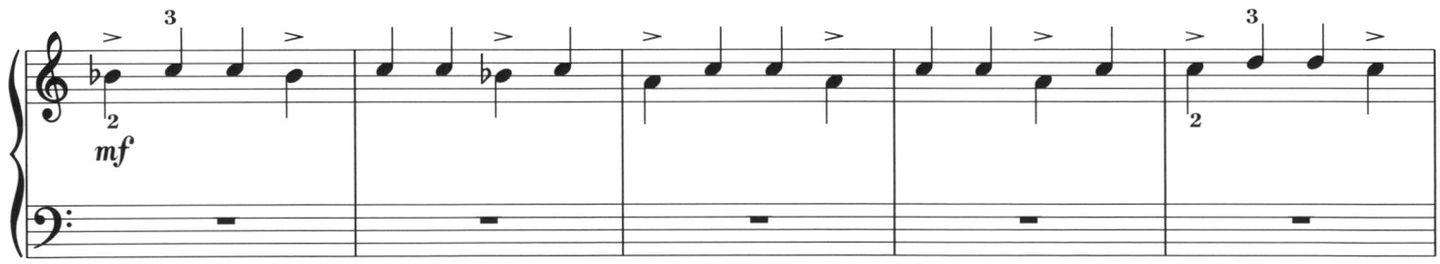

Honk! honk!

Roderick Skeaping

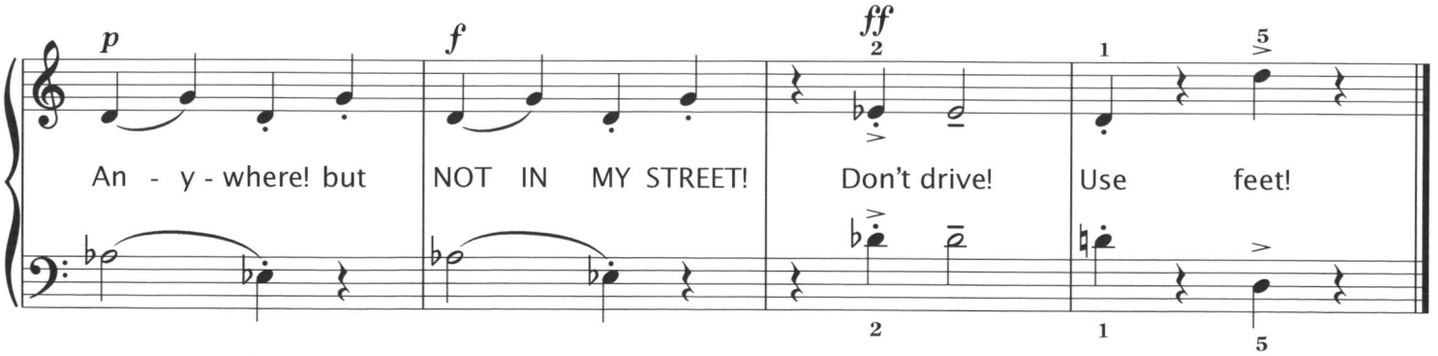

Penny-farthing

Tempo di minuetto (𝅗𝅥. = *c.*56)

Alan Bullard

p

f

mf

f

ff

A swim in crocodile river

David Cullen

Mexican march

David Cullen

Moderato (♩ = 112)

f

p

f

p

f

ff

Paris promenade

David Cullen

Moderate swing (♩ = 132)

mf

1. 2.

mp

cresc.

mf

cresc.

f

The train

Roderick Skeaping

Expectantly

p

Rail track's hum-ming, mail train's com-ing, Woooo! Woooo!

Ped.

pp cresc. poco a poco

Lis-ten to the hum-ming rail and you will hear the morn-ing mail train.

huff-ing puff-ing chuff-ing puff-ing huff-ing puff-ing chuff-ing puff-ing

mp As it flies past *f* gra - zing cat - tle

Ped.

huff-ing puff-ing chuff-ing puff-ing huff-ing puff-ing chuff-ing puff-ing

mp whis - tle shrieks and *f* coach - es rat - tle.

Ped.

cresc.

Now the sound is get - ting clear - er as the steam train's puff - ing near - er.

sempre f
rall.
Dri - ver sees the sig - nal low - er;
pulls the brake: 'She's get - ting slow - er!'
Grinding to a halt . . .
Till she stops in - side the sta - tion,
on her way a - cross the na - tion.
a tempo
lunga
Woooo!
Woooo!
pp
Santa Lucia
Italian song
Pauline Hall
Slow waltz time
p smoothly
simile
mf

Allegro (♩ = 132)

f

mp

mf

f

The bluebottle's last journey

S. Watt

Two in tandem

Primo right hand an octave higher throughout.

Alan Bullard

f
f
p
p
f
f

mf
f
mf
f

ff
ff